# The Zoo

Prairie Schooner Book Prize in Poetry
EDITOR Kwame Dawes

# at Night

Susan Gubernat

University of Nebraska Press

LINCOLN AND LONDON

Library of Congress Cataloging-in-Publication Data
Names: Gubernat, Susan, 1949– author.
Title: The zoo at night / Susan Gubernat.
Description: Lincoln: University of Nebraska Press, [2017] |
Series: Prairie Schooner Book Prize in poetry
Identifiers: LCCN 2017010430 (print) | LCCN 2017013370 (ebook)
ISBN 9781496202055 (pbk.: alk. paper)
ISBN 9781496202758 (epub)
ISBN 9781496202765 (mobi)
ISBN 9781496202772 (pdf)
Classification: LCC PS3557.U234 (ebook) | LCC PS3557.
U234 A6 2017 (print) | DDC 811/.54—dc23
LC record available at https://lccn.loc.gov/2017010430

Set in Quadraat by John Klopping.
Designed by N. Putens.

# CONTENTS

## III

## IV

## V

## ACKNOWLEDGMENTS

My thanks to the editors of the following publications in which versions of these poems originally appeared:

*Cimarron Review:* "Fonder"
*Confrontation:* "Sharing a Birthday with Mata Hari"
*Corner Pocket:* "The Buddhas of Bamiyan"
*The Cortland Review:* "Etruscans"
*Crab Orchard Review:* "The Roosevelt"
*Gargoyle:* "I Was In Gym Class When Cronkite Said They'd Shot
    Him"; "Reading Loop: The Sibyl at Cumae"
*Lullwater Review:* "Poster Children"
*The Meadow:* "Blue Tooth"
*The Michigan Quarterly Review:* "Hats, Purses, Gloves"; "Feather
    Duster"; "Ground Note"
*The Pinch:* "The Fascicles of Emily Dickinson"; "Pears in Winter"
*Parthenon West Review:* "The Right Hand of Goltzius"
*Pleiades:* "The Singer"; "Easter Bread"; "Hades"
*Poemeleon:* "Ground Time"
*Prairie Schooner:* "Wedding Cookies"; "On a Scale Of"
*Scoundrel Time:* "My Sister and I Are Having the Same Dream";
    "Report a Problem with This Poem"
*Spillway:* "Shaggy Parasol"
*Stand (UK):* "Deathbed Proof"; "'Beautiful Contrivances' in the
    Sex Life of Orchids"; "Day Lilies"
*The Texas Review:* "Winter Coats"
*The Yalobusha Review:* "Too Soon"

*Analog House: A Cabinet of Curiosities* first appeared in chapbook form, published by Finishing Line Press.

Special thanks to the Virginia Center for the Creative Arts, the Corporation of Yaddo, the MacDowell Colony, and the Millay Colony for the space and seed time needed for this poetry to grow. I'm indebted to California State University, East Bay; in particular, I'm most grateful for the support of the students and colleagues who have helped nurture my work. Eternal gratitude is due to Drs. Susan Sherman and Karla Clark, who have been its midwives. To my dear friends—East and West—great love and affection, as I travel restlessly back and forth between the coasts. And finally, to Mark, who has been the still point in the turning world.

The Zoo at Night

I

# Etruscans

The woman, wool-capped, filthy, knelt beside
a man asleep at the curb, so tenderly—
well, what can I say but that I envied
them in my full belly. I've never wrapped
my chest in newspaper or begged for change
with a Styrofoam cup or slept on the street.
And I welled up with self-pity: I'm safe,
I'm warm, I'm alone. My donor's card reads:
Take the whole body, the body entire,
leave nothing behind for burial. The stone couples
lean against each other, and in the tomb
a queen's dust merges with her king's—the sweet,
the bitter, an apothecary's mixture
to salve the horror of eternity.

# Wedding Cookies

Don't tell me to love this world,
its surfeit of sweetness: lacy pizzelles,
dollops of anisette drops,
ladyfingers, lady locks, nipples of Venus
piled on a wedding tray like hundreds
of virgin martyrs, undone.

Cinching the bomb to her waist, the girl
has this request—to clench
a sugar cube in her teeth
as she drains her tea to the dregs.

I once had a cache of silver dollars
spent as soon as my mother handed
my dowry over. What was there
to save for? I planned to die young.

So I get this girl, her rush to oblivion.

Weddings, funerals, and all the births
in between, old women cooing,
blood on the sheets like raspberry jam
drying to chocolate, ginger men
made limbless, torsos snapped in two.

Then, there are those Jordan almonds
favored at weddings: bittersweet,
slick white bullets wrapped in gauze
to put under your pillow. And dream
of something new, some other world.

# The Right Hand of Goltzius

*The Metropolitan Museum of Art*

He had fallen into the fire,
a baby then—the kind of
sixteenth-century kitchen
accident that maimed him
for life, torqued the hand
into a useless caliper,
where, as it happened,
he most needed
to be lithe and free.

From such disfigurement
came an engraver's
exacting figures:
striated loins of pagan gods
and heroes, fretted tableaux
of the Virgin's life, a taut
and tensile study of
the twisted fingers
of his own right hand
not the least of these,
and the exhibition's centerpiece.

So we celebrate
the romance of recovery,
enshrined in a curator's cure
for ennui. Nothing's impossible,
yes, yes, we already know. Just
think of what can be done

armless, a brush clutched

between the toes, the teeth.

Then why am I not comforted?
Not inspired, not raised up.

When Dolores on the street,
homeless, exchanges my money
for her story, unbidden—
she's less nauseated from
chemo today, the tumors
are shrinking, she has to get
back to her "babies" now, as if
she might grind their food
in her toothless mouth,
pierce her rotting flesh to feed them—

all I can think is how Goltzius,
burin in his good left hand,
also made these:
A series of engravings of naked
hubrists, each tumbling, solitary,
into the void—Phaeton, Icarus,
viewed from behind, too late,
limbs flailing decorously: powerful,
useless musculature in free fall.

*Show me the sparrow, Lord. Show me the tree.*

# I Was in Gym Class When Cronkite Said They'd Shot Him

Last night the party boat blazed in Reynolds
Channel, like the birthday cake they spent days
decorating for J F K, and then,
when the waiters carried it out on a huge tray,
wobbling between them, all you could think is
oh god, they'll drop it—the way you feared
Marilyn's dress would split open at those straining
seams he must have run his finger down. "Well," as
students say when they take up a topic
reluctantly on the page, they're both reruns
anyway: The drawbridge cranks open
every night for the gamblers' homecoming,
win or lose. The ship glides through, still lit
up. All a little silly really, faux naïve in its
moue of girlish expectation. Go on, honey, blow.

# Sharing a Birthday with Mata Hari

She refused the blindfold, faced twelve raised guns,
men's erections so familiar to her
she blew them a kiss before the last captain
emptied his charge into her ear to ensure
her death. Already dead now, wasn't she?
And in the arms of Shiva. In prison
she'd grown blowsy on the starches they fed
her. And rank—the small bowl of water
she'd bathe with was as paltry as the handkerchief
a woman dabs at her sweaty neck in August,
in the Jardin du Luxembourg. Never
had she danced naked, made love naked,
but hid her tiny breasts behind a metal
breastplate she'd stuff for all occasions,
claiming McLeod, the husband, had bitten
her nipples off. Oh, we are never beautiful enough.

I know, she told the nuns who flanked her,
how to face my death. What a triptych
they must have made, such a procession
of virgin-whore-virgin, making their way
to the prison courtyard. Once they'd stopped,
indicating her mark, did they even offer her
the dignity of a cigarette?

This isn't about knowledge, confirmed, denied:
stale, useless facts. But it is about betrayal,
as you'd expect. A former lover at her trial
bowed low to her, saying there was no cause.

No cause. Nevertheless, there must be stoning.
Such a woman cannot walk among us
unless she's freed to stand her redemptive
vigil at the foot of some cross, and not to re-join
her new young lover, the age of a lost son.

I think it might have been the embalmer, working
with what was left, who first saw Mata Hari's breasts,
her once-perfect little breasts.

# Atlantic City

The Steel Pier (which implies forever)
must have gripped the sandy bottom
harder than the lady rider held on,
diving into a tank of water, bareback,
on a dark horse, her shorn head like
a cannonball, or her tresses smoothed
ballistically by a tight bathing cap
that pulled her eyebrows up
into a permanent askance.
What in the world . . . ? The housewives
watching the act fought the thrill
that welled up below the waist
for the first time in weeks.

2

A family outing: he, smelling
of roasted peanuts and melting
Dairy Queen. Squirmy children
ranged between them
on the splinter-making wooden
seats, agape as a row of water-gun
clowns—the boardwalk game
the wife could always win, expert
at aiming liquid into any open mouth.

3

The chute opened, the rider
urged her steed down. With what
steely spurs or animal memory
of a sweet reward? They rode the air

together like the Sidhe. But once
in the barrel, knocked about
like proverbial fish, easy prey.

4

A child begged for the restroom,
and suddenly they were driving
north, home. In the front seat,
she reached for the nape of his neck
and he flinched, then relaxed
at something nearly familiar.

5

Last dive of the day:
on her little stage, the rider
was coaxing her mount again,
nuzzling his mane. While around them
the Atlantic slapped at the pillars
driven so deep they had entered
the mermaids' chambers.

# Smart Enough

You can only get so far, smart girl, I'm telling
my dear old self, until the mind crumbles
like stale bread left to mark the trail
and, anyway, the birds have scarfed
it all up. Filthy things. But they have to eat.

And whether, reluctantly, you feed the gulls
diving at the ferry rails, hovering in midair,
white paper kites on a lucky March wind,
or refuse to share with the Canada geese
that overstay their welcome now, leaving
their gray-green stools around the lake
(small, abandoned works in clay never
to be annealed by flames in the kiln),
you too, like them, will fade away.

Already you're not so sharp, your edges
beveled with a strange kindness
for the woman who hobbles ahead
of you in line, hip out of joint
and poised now, waiting for her pills
in the pharmacy—wretched egret
smiling back at you when
you didn't even know that you were smiling.

But the caucus race is on: to discover which
is first to fail—mind or body. Surprised
that you are loath to choose, then shamed
at the mind's impertinence,
its false exercise of will.

*Nyah, nyah, smart girl!*

When I was a toddler, terrified
of nearly everything, an aunt
and uncle kept a parakeet named Chico
that swooped at children's heads,
sipped water from a china cup,
and dirtied all the valences when let out
of his cage. Then he died, and I was safe.

Or so I thought. They soon bought another bird.
And called him Chico.

# The Roosevelt

There, in its prewar splendor, purple plush of seat cushions
    chafed to a kind of worn glory, like an old dame
playing Hamlet: the neighborhood theatre we walked past daily—
    forbidden to us, even as other children's Saturdays, logy
with soda and sweets, passed in a bland euphoria of cartoons,
    horror movies, and, later, practice-kissing amid smells
of urine and Pine-Sol and burnt popcorn. Forbidden, except
    for "classics" and Bible stories: The Ten Commandments and Ben-Hur
from which I gleaned enough sexual fantasy to last me years: Heston's
    bare chest, Stephen Boyd's villainous cleft chin, or even
the thrill of Pinocchio's being swallowed by the whale until he built
    a fire inside the leviathan. A few doors down was the dress shop
where my aunts got measured by an old woman driven out of Europe,
    like the shoemaker who scowled at us when handing over
our newly-heeled oxfords in a wrinkled paper bag. I was told
    my great-grandmother had willed herself to live long enough
to see FDR assume a fourth term in office. Still, in the old album's
    photographs she most resembled Fraulein Rottenmeier in Heidi,
and I was glad she was dead so I'd have nothing to do with her.
    I could admire her politics, admire too the others who hid
a whole family during a pogrom in Poland. We were that kind
    of Catholic, I could tell myself—though I knew I'd be forbidden
to graze the lips of a Jewish boy with my lips. And so would he.

# Christmas Fires

Dragged down by the weight of ornament,
a tree starts sizzling in the arid house
while the family sleeps, each child
holding a new gift tightly to her chest.

Or is it a mutant candle flame wavering
then licking the edge of the votive glass
like an old man searching for gristle
at the back of his mouth?

The fire engine hauling Santa through
the neighborhoods last week (balanced
illicitly on a ladder, four beers into it)
now cuts through the night's
space-time continuum: before and after.

And everyone in new bedroom slippers
picking their way across iced-over pavement
toward an ugly epiphany: bodies in blankets
not their own rolled out of the smoke
on silver wheels that wobble
across crusts of blackened snow.

I knew a woman who smoked in bed
and died of such burns after much suffering—
she, the solitary who used to watch us
recite our prayers on Christmas Eve and then
retire to her drafty room, her movie magazines,
the smoldering cigarette, its tip aglow
like the first star of evening.

I'm saying all this to remind myself of the great
loneliness we share, of hooves stamping
the barn floor—a random sound, without cadence,
even if, on the quiet road, one stops to listen.

# Winter Coats

The first layer of snow still clings to the tall
grasses as if to a mare's winter coat,
that long-haired horse in the photo you pinned
up near your desk. I never understood
the image, why it moved you so—creased, rough-edged
icon among the few in your spare but
messy room. Was it "cold comfort," clichéd
oxymoron you'd revel in, in secret?
I learned to miss you while I lived with you
and visited that photograph instead,
like the child who leaves adults to their bright,
brittle dinner talk, and buries her face in piles
of the cold, wet fur they left behind on the bed.

# After the Abortion

*For J.K.*

A wasp built under the eaves, the threshold
you'd cross a hundred times a day into the garden
to tug at the carrot's fine green lace
in your impatience; to split cordwood,
setting your half-burned cigarette on a flat log
as you braced yourself and struck at the heart;
to gossip with Henry, whom we had lured
out of all his Yankee recalcitrance
to our side of the fence once or twice
simply by working so hard. Above our heads
the wasp worked too, spinning a vessel
smooth as wet clay.
        How rarely on those sultry days
I found my favorite potter in his workshop:
he trusted us to take just what we wanted
and leave the cash in a jar too cracked
even for "seconds." It had its uses.
There were always rows of plates and bowls
piled up before firing, the color of a wasp's nest,
a kind of parchment gray. The Neoplatonist
in me would say those forms were as anonymous
as souls. But why wouldn't the potter show
his own face now and then? All I had of him
was the mark he pressed into what he'd made,
a fingernail dent in the rim, but a sign
nonetheless. Something arcane. Buddhist?

2

The Japanese build shrines for their aborted ones:
*mizuko jizo*, "water babies"—clay figurines

inscribed with names and visited often, clothed
sometimes like dolls, doused with water ritually
in a mourning that goes on quite apart from what
we know as guilt. Infantile as it seemed,
I would have liked to build a shrine. And told you so
on Crotched Mountain where we only fingered
the dusty berries of the juniper, crushing them
for the sharp smell of gin, rolled wild blueberries
into our mouths, then descended without repentance.

3

For weeks I had watched the wasp build, indefatigable,
watched your comings and goings in fear, in revenge—
your bee-sting kit cinched to your belt, allergy
serum ready in its neat syringe against anaphylaxis,
the horrors of a closing throat, a brain gone blank
as a tablet. Insistent wasp, she nested in her opaque
paper lantern until the night I made a move:
I sprayed poison up into that hardened little room,
took a broom handle to it, knocked it onto the grass.
And once I sensed no stirring there, I shattered it.

# Shaggy Parasol

Bone white and thrusting up from the loam,
a foot high and terrible, a nightmare mushroom—
or a child's idea of one, the way these round hills
resemble a child's first crayoned hills (the child
who's never seen one). You say to pull it up
is a kind of desecration and with a swift knife
slice it from the earth where it will grow again.
The underside is pleated neatly, over and over,
tiny bellows, an ivory fan. You say we'll eat it.
With such authority, such determination—I succumb.
I decide you are a wise old man and not a pompous
pedant hiking in a string shirt like a market bag,
chuffy, and chafing at my headlong pace,
my will to blaze a trail alone. When the last
sliver slips between my teeth, onto my tongue,
golden from its sizzling bath of oil, I bow
to you, admonished, bow beneath the small
shelter it once made in the woods. How much
I would have missed by forging on, living,
as I have lived, archly, and without trust.

II

# Analog House

## A Cabinet of Curiosities

# The Singer

Treadle pumping, the tiny light of the machine
haloed folds in the fabric, its resistance
smoothed, then coaxed under the needle's eye
by her meaty hand as the shuttle engaged,
withdrew. Engaged. Withdrew. And again
and again, my dark fantasy of fingertips pierced
and sewn together, like lips. Shirring, rickrack,
loose basting by hand, straight pins poking
out of her mouth, grim against swallowing.
Nor did anyone else make a sound.
The rubber atomizer puffed chalk dust
for hems while she shimmied around us
on knees, on shins, as at the icon's unveiling,
the scarred, blackened virgin and child.

# Easter Bread

Wooden spatula folding the brown veins
of cinnamon into the yeast bread
that had risen, sweaty, under a white cloth,
the dough cleaving, undulating,
turning over like a great dreamer
under the earth. Red-tipped match
striking up a blue flame in the firebox
just after a whiff of gas—so sweet
when it rested like that on the windowsill
before dispersing into the back lot dubbed
"vacant" once the Victory gardens had
bolted. The oil trucks rolled in
over the scattered seed. The seal
on the last mason jar had been broken.

# Hades

It took the coal man and all his sons
a long summer morning to back their truck
into the alley, slide the metal chutes
through the slit cellar windows, hooked wide
open, for once, and send tons of black clods
clattering into the bins. A single piece
of their coal was almost weightless, shiny
as a patent leather shoe, unstrapped,
dangling from a little girl's toe.
But the roar! As if the fires had escaped
without consuming the bowels of the house.
There they lay, glinting like an old man's dark
mouth when he remembers winter,
cold floors, how she couldn't deny him then.

# Doberman

Like your grandfather but he was no one's
grandfather, and what language did he speak?
We never heard him. Maybe in his country
he had been the tax collector who needed
that Doberman, coat the color of dried blood,
and the walking stick he swished and raised,
sometimes, over the dog's head. Willow wand,
I think, in his country, where he would douse
for water on Sundays, slip the choke chain
off the animal's neck, ride him bareback
into the new streams he had coaxed up.
I never heard his switch land on the Doberman
but I saw the dog cower in the curb,
make his obeisance to the sewers.

# Meat Grinder

You fed the funnel hocks of it, raw,
and it streamed out in prim ribbons, not quite
flesh anymore. Or you could let the butcher
take this part away from you, lay the wax
paper on a scale, make it a matter
of pure weight. Just a little over what
you'd ordered. But I wanted to watch it
extrude into her open palm or bowl
she held out like a midwife. She'd sculpt a loaf
by stroking the sides into a squared mound
like those ancient queens must have humped
from the earth to live in; or she'd mold buckshot
dwarves for us to feast on, rolled one by one
and shoved into fluted pockets, pinched shut.

# Piano Bench

It creaks when opened slowly, when opened
swiftly, smells like the inside of an old
lady's hatbox. When closed—mazurkas tap
fingers against the lid like a coffin
of the undead. What purpose does it serve
with the piano gone? Once it was too high
for the pedals; now you can stand on it,
to reach the shelf of Christmas ornaments.
Ah, that's a happy memory, isn't it?
Switch on the record player, gently
place the needle near the edge. A tiny pop
like a party favor, and the crooner
starts caroling. No need to sing along.
Just listen. Stop drumming on the table.

# 13th Fairy

Bring on the cake! Freon-laced buttercream
swirled like cockle shells. Then, more lies about
wishing before the candles have been snuffed
by her asbestos fingers—she can take
the fire away from anything. A boy's tongue
has morphed into a pink paper dragon
stretching, then rolling back into his mouth.
Under tents of gaudy wrap, new school clothes
are folded into fresh white boxes. Next: thunder,
not so distant now. Windows slammed and latched
against summer rain, the afternoon sky
cracks like stemware, the cramped room is sweating
in electric light. All are melting, melting
back into witches beneath their peaked hats.

# Washboard

Knuckle-scraper, hoarse and scratchy lyre,
cha CHA-cha, cha CHA-cha. They laid their rings
aside on laundry day, even the flawless
small diamond set in platinum. Cha-CHA.
So as to be reminded nothing was
compensatory, preferring river
rocks and gossip to this solitary
work, forgetting too when they scrubbed a child's
sticky mouth how tender he was, how strong
their wrists had grown, fooled by their own
flimsy housedresses. I've watched a Cajun
play the board, hung against his naked chest,
craving that rough touch, nipple abrasion,
fingers that could ravish a mandolin.

# Clothesline

Hand over hand—and sopping sheets and towels,
the underclothes, even ragged ones, sport
themselves before the morning commuters.
Nothing to hide, or everything to hide
when you can reach out over the alley
and finger the neighbors at their dinner.
Blown about in the half-light of winter,
cinder-specked, all clothes are gathered back in
when shades are drawn to the sills. Even so,
streetlights leak in, car beams. And once the fierce
flapping of laundry comes to rest, disheveled
in stiff baskets, groans and slaps of evening
distract the child at prayer, her small hands steepled,
hoisting sail to catch the last good wind.

# Feather Duster

Molted to near baldness it still wielded
Aztec powers as if the sun would emerge
only in a mote-hung universe. Dirt
never disappeared. Neither created
nor destroyed, so long as we failed to eat
our ancestors. And we laughed at the line
"That's me all over" every time Scarecrow
tried stuffing himself back in, apoplectic.
Though my wastrel uncle had knocked out
a tooth or two from her head before she threw
him out for good, my aunt do-ragged it up
on the weekend, cleaned the living daylights
out of that house, redistributing dirt
with a feather duster, bird thou never wert.

# Spirit Level

What could we do but measure ourselves
and be found wanting? The straight shall be made
crooked. But I was a cock-eyed optimist
for a time, convinced the air bubble would hit
the exact spot: equanimity. Souls
can do no better. You only needed
tools, and we had them. Voices and minds, willing.
Place it down on the cold ground, in the midst
of a city crowd, a slick corridor
of power. And it will list and founder. Try
again: it will disappear. Off the chart.
He had a roomful of tools that couldn't
save him in the end. My father rode it
like a dolphin and drowned. Mind over matter.

# Paint-by-Number

Follow numbers, stay within the lines and
it's a sure thing, like other people's puzzles
glued together and hung up. A certain
mystery attended them and you could flout
directions: exchange a blue lake for a blue
tree. Make the lake red, the barn black.
Particularly if you'd never seen
barns or lakes. Trees were in short supply. Before
the eye exam I thought of leaves as swaths
of green, indistinguishable. Unique?
A vocabulary word. Mispronounced
in three Latin syllables. As at Mass:
the priest broke apart the host and then God
reconnected the dots. Voilà! the painting.

# Net

Off the spider's loom and against her nape,
a hair net kept the strays in place under
the pretense of invisibility.
She had forsaken the bold snood of the war
years for this fragile purse seine, one that trapped
her errancy, and fixed the Celtic swirl
of hair at her neck—but some pins wriggled
out as daylight ebbed. Vanity, saith
the preacher; she sat before the mirror,
releasing the catch from the tortoiseshell
and it spilled onto her shoulders, a weir
bursting. Cast aside amidst a cargo
of vials—Djer Kiss, Prince Machiabelli,
Tabu—the net seized up, a doused spider.

# Netting

A baby carriage left unattended
invites cats. The jump-in, smothering kind.
Mosquito netting was the least a mother
could do anent the world's pests, the stinging
kind, while up four flights for a fresh bottle,
its lukewarm pearls shaken onto her wrist,
as though the bound breasts wept. Then down again
before the infant woke up beneath
cheesecloth, in a ferment certain to disturb
the neighbors who much preferred a solemn
unveiling. Though not today: the carriage
brake has lost its grip and all have rolled—
buggy, baby with thumb—into the street,
path of the fuming bus, netting intact.

# Hats, Purses, Gloves

Respectable, as the mothers of poor
little girls yearn for them to be, measured
by Easter finery, is what we must have been.
Jaunty, even, in fake straw and ribbons,
in T-strapped patent leather, ankle socks
we tugged at all the bleak morning of one
of Christ's many resurrections. We hid
eggs beneath banisters, under cellar doors,
took fevered communion. Not a grass blade
in the oil-soaked lot, not a snowdrop. Buds
poked out on rose bushes as if feeling
for a new tooth. The aunt we most despised
clutched us to her perfumed linen suit topped
by foxes gnawing at each other's tails.

# Vestibule

Neither here nor there: all expectation.
As the mailman's key turns in the brass lock
the stiff boxes come unhinged like tongues.
How it smells of everyone but yourselves—
of furniture polish and grass tracked in,
of cardboard, damp wool, the doctor's aftershave.
The outer door is heavy with beveled
glass so that, on the edges, every face
distorts as in a funhouse. This isn't
fun. From here, all the loose dogs on the street
appear rabid; the stranger keeps wanting
to get in, in. You're sure he won't until
from above someone answers his sharp buzz.
A click. And he stands in the hall beside you.

# Deliberate Happiness

> No one denies to Keats love of the world:
> Remember his deliberate happiness.
> . . . His art is happy, but who knows his mind?
> I see a schoolboy when I think of him,
> With face and nose pressed to a sweet-shop window . . .
>
> W. B. Yeats, "Ego Dominus Tuus"

Filthy corner store for bread, for cigarettes,
it throve, in fact, on penny candy behind
glass, Keatsian urge for a bit of sweetness
between the hour milk bottles chimed
on the landing, filled at the top with cream
that disappeared, and the hour the possum
hoisted her low-slung paps onto the street.
Oyster sky. Pigeon sky. We tugged away
at licorice strings, sucked the sugar buttons
off streamers so fiercely we swallowed
paper. Paper, I said, I need paper,
the night they caught me sleepwalking. She heated
milk in a porcelain pot. It frothed and spilled
into my mouth—beaker full of the warm South.

# Photo on Pony

Knife-grinder; vegetable peddler; the man
with cameras panniered on his pony's
flanks to take our pictures. We dealt with them
in kind. Make the dull sharp enough to peel
his peaches, ripening in brown paper.
Make us beautiful on horses. From the porch
she'd answer the suitors' street cries. *Missus,*
*what do you like? Got tomatoes, four pounds*
*for a quarter. Got fresh sweet corn. Got. Got.*
They sent bad boys to the farms for theft,
for slashing another boy's wrist. I saw
him run through the schoolyard, bleeding;
the other was wielding a kitchen knife,
after him, still. Mister, take your best shot.

# Underwood in Flames

*After Leopoldo Maler's* Hommage *(1974)*

What's missing in this near-silent clicking:
the necessary exertion to know
you're working—that whole type carriage shifting
to mark a capital on the page: O
rises up in its fully empty form,
or halves itself like Kilroy's boasting head
saying: I was here too, before the last worm
finished me off. Out sick from school, instead
of lessons I spent my long slow hours touch-
typing. The Underwood out of storage,
its black, leathery, cubic coffin such
an anomaly in her kitchen. The page
was white as her porcelain stove until
I charred it with the fires of my will.

# III

# The Zoo at Night (1)

Many will write of the tiger attack,
of those young men taunting her.
But I will write about you,
foreswearing the easy metaphor
of the unpredictable pent-up beast,
metonyms of tooth and claw

because the mere violence of your eye,
non-swipe of your paw,
were most unnatural, Mother.

And I could carry my raw
penitence and place it at your feet
having plucked the worms from it myself,
swallowed them whole. And still

you wouldn't eat. Isn't it the child,
tight-lipped, refusing to feed,
who consternates the mother?

Instead it was me, prodding your mouth
with the tip of a spoon
I could barely wield until
you opened wide a jaw

more like a lower creature's—
an insect or green carnivore

not walled in or moated,
fenced, restrained behind bars,
but growing luxuriant in that garden
we once called home.

# Aphasia of the Moon

In the sky, a cuticle moon, a white eyelash.
Waning moon: tightened smile of the old woman, old man
our parents have become. Still, they have all

their teeth, rotting to pieces now in his skull
as he refuses to brush them, a petulant child again,
and hers, ready to snap at us, wolverine,

hyena-mother. One by one, the forms fall away
and we are rendered animal, blood and bone
on which the weary flesh depends. Rim-of-saucer moon

from which he sips his spilled tea. Curled-edge-
of-a-songbook moon, from which she'll never play again.
Soon, the new moon's blankness will fill it all in,

the black crayon a daughter would never dare
reach for in this box of greasy colors, pointedly.
Instead, she trusts the sun to coax the blues and greens

even as her mother coaxes her father from their bed
each morning and back again at night
when he is most the moon, the pursed-lip moon, not speaking,
this absent presence, this invisible drag on the tides.

# Sick Child

A clean, warm rag snugged against the throat,
a mother's poultice made with VapoRub.
When she gets to California, breathes its herb-rich air,
she will think of her, that balm of eucalyptus
for the awful coughing. And how the lamp was dimmed
with a scarf so the room still held some light,
just enough to brush shadows onto the wall
with dark finger paints, easy on the eyes.

Sickly children know at once both comfort and despair
while the others scream down icy hills on sleds,
or, fearless astride shaky handlebars, plow
right into one another and, roughed-up, wear
their scabs like badges. All her bones in place,
she trolled Anderson and Grimm, wheezing, a tablet
under the tongue, toast and tea, fevered dreaming.

Such reading—antidote to loneliness,
protracted soothing when food and medicine
would fail. She did her sums alone, no class
reciting, in the folds of a flowered bedspread.
Ever after, her sheets have been scarred
by pencil and pen. And like some little queen,
she expects honey now for every bitter drink.

# Filia

The clear thin tubing sinks into both nostrils
so that the low wind can reach her. The old woman
stands in a long line of passengers thumbing
their crumpled plane reservations, while the daughter
behind her holds the canister of air she's breathing,
touching her shoulder lightly, as if to say,
*Move on, love,* as the line moves.

          But I can't reach you, mom,
across this expanse of sky over the cold Sierras,
corduroy plains, Amish farmhouses tucked
into the landscape, even if I wanted to.
And anyway, I might shove you along,
secretly pleased you'd have to raise both arms
for the metal detector, armed and dangerous
as you were. I would ask them to frisk you,
do a cavity search, and find me there: girl-child
about to be born. I'd say *Confiscate me. Seize me.*
*Please, take me away from her.* Make all my orphan
fantasies, even now, come true.

          The line moves.
The daughter holds her mother's box of breath
like a reliquary or a treasure chest excavated
from some saint's tomb. Good daughter, she
expects it holds nothing, and that is enough.

# Poster Children

*For Tobias Schneebaum*

Today I wanted to save all the dogs from being,
what do they say, "put down"? In a week
they'll kill Star, the sweet collie mix,
her close-up Polaroid beseeching.
She's eager. I know that eagerness.
As well as Rufus of the spiked collar,
liver-colored gums—he's looking askance,
is all I can call it, at the shelter's
photographer, who must have urged
an empathy-inducing flinch. Nothing
doing: beware the teeth.
              And we agree:
Neither of us can bring them home.
You travel the world—Singapore,
the Yucatán, places like Rio where
hairless pink dogs abound, none
of them yours. Besides, you have
eaten dogs, or worse.
              My last mongrel
was ceded to the lover I learned to despise.
He seemed kinder than I, likelier
to live in the suburbs. She was terrified
of pavements, grew constipated around
curbs. I foisted shame onto her,
I know, when she'd shit in public places.

That night we watched
*The 400 Blows* together, I thought
I would rail against narcissists until dawn.
How dare they turn into parents?
Instead of children, I've found dogs I could abandon.

# La Sebastiana

On her cheek a tiny silver bead, a cake decoration—
but how can metal be so oddly sweet? She sighs
and sucks it, hard, into another layer of skin,
her linen face mottled. And the eyes—the eyes
repeat, "Please help me" but look elsewhere,
anything to distract them: glint of the tin
foil of gum wrapper ground into the floor,
tree shadow on window shade this late afternoon.

She's confessing to me about her father.
Who knew the world was so full of them,
easing open the doors of daughters' rooms?
So many girls keeping the secret, who scar
their arms and thighs, pierce the most tender skin,
these tribal marks on ears, nose, lips, tongue saying,

*I own my own body, see, I mark it again and again.*

# Portrait at Fourteen

*Monterey Bay Aquarium*

Foghorns blow, and what of the boy who looks
forward to . . . reincarnation as a seal?!
He admires lolling, the creature's roll
into the bay off a guano-stained rock
where its meals wait, off-handedly. Basted
and sand-crumbed on the beach, fine seal blubber
resists the pressure to be limber;
no black-belt sparring, career counseling, SATs.
Beyond breakfast lies lunch. Then, dinner.
Darkly, through aquarium glass, his gaze rides
the bottom feeders and not the silver school
of anchovies, that centrifuge of glittering toil
in such perpetual motion, wasted—
a thousand penknives thrown against the tide.

# Ground Time

My friend the harpist, a swami who read my palm before I took off again for the unknown, said, *Children will always be drawn to you; you have been a mother many times. But not in this life.* As the plane plows to a halt, its wings flap open to reveal the bolts and screws that have kludged our flight. In the seat ahead of me, a big-faced baby with tufted hair screams as if to match the roar. Then the anonymous, department-store bell. Then the silence that requires some speech, finally, between passengers: *Nice flight. Where are you headed?* And even I accept *Have a good day* from the baby's family traveling on to the Cascades—a reunion. I tell them that their baby gets the prize for being best baby on the flight, avoiding gender terms because I can't tell—the clothes too hip to provide a clue. Emboldened, their other child, a fantastically braided girl, starts asking me where and when, and it gets so close now in this airless cabin I fear her inquiring next about my absent children. While I could take her sister's (or brother's) face in my hands and nearly crush it with love, so hungry for the puckered mouth, the ardent gaze of nursing. But the baby must be past that now, as am I. And how could anyone lay away someone else's eggs in her womb? How could the sitter surrender her charge at noon, nape just damp from napping, then watch him shinny up the ladder-back to get a grip on his mother's neck, anoint the top of her head with sticky kisses? I am dangerous to myself around children—as dangerous as the woman who drowned all five of hers, like cats, in a warm bath. (God, how do you hold a seven-year-old under?) I kidnap them all in my head, mine the gaze of predation. I've skipped diapers and pre-dawn feedings and fever, arriving at this: Mine, the best baby on the Earhart flight, under the radar, off the charts, churning in the horse latitudes; the dream-baby gathered in from the fire escape; the snow-suited astronaut tethered to the air.

# No Warrior

*Whaddya gonna do?* My father's mantra.
And did he shrug or raise his arms to heaven?
I can't remember. But when the other man
in my life disappeared from the city for weeks,
then from a phone booth called to say
he loved both me and another (and he was with her)
I reached for my father, weeping before him

as I hadn't done since the iron merry-go-round
I'd leapt for, and missed, dragged me
along the ground through gravel. And my mother
had to tweeze each black shard from my knees
while my father shaved or drank the cup
of tea his own mother poured for him,
clucking at his fate.
                    Strings slackened,
he couldn't cross the room to touch me.

And as I tried fording at the deepest place
to meet him, the coin fell out of my mouth,
all illusion of psychopomp withdrew—oh,
and I knew that in life, in death,
ahead of shield there would always be shadow.

# The Collective

## A Clutter of Spiders

You are never far from a spider, he says,
so I look up and
there's the gray trail
like ancient threads
of a wedding dress
hanging from the ceiling.
There's the red mark
on his naked chest
to reveal he'd been bitten
in the night, and not by me.
How the past sticks
like spider spit
to our dreams.

## A Clutch of Chicks

There was that Easter
I barely remember, when
the yellow chick hopped
from its cardboard box and bolted
under the stove where it was warm
again, like a mother hen. My mother
said she had to get rid of it then,
terrified, she said, she'd step on it.
At three, I made her pack my bag
so I could run away.

## A Nuisance of Cats

The kitten wound yarn around her neck,
around the table leg, and pulled until

she nearly choked to death; from that litter
her brother too was suicidal, nearly
plunging from the window ledge.
Or so I thought until I read
of the fortunate cat that fell nineteen floors
to a safe landing on all four paws.
And so I kept going.

## A Flamboyance of Flamingos

Humid excess, this alliterative brood,
impossible stalks and necks, worse
narcissists, even, than swans—
always primping, beaks rummaging
among their own feathers. To fly
they need a running start.
Spiked heels, platform shoes hobble
the beautiful skinny girls
whose bird legs buckle, whose ankles
turn, and ruffled, undone,
they crash on runways around the world.

## A Wake of Buzzards

In the canyon something has left
its life behind, gone to ground,
skin sizzling in the noonday heat.
And here they come, first circling
in a contra dance of patterns in high air,
signaling—as the guests approached
the coffin where my father lay:
no one makes a beeline for it.
No, they ride the air streams in the room,
invisible currents holding them aloft
until entropy, its hunger,
brings them closer for a taste.

### A Charm of Hummingbirds

So easy to please: just sugar water
or a bright-red flower (fuchsia, hibiscus)
they can dip their beaks in,
hovering while their gauzy
wings beat furiously.
Just call me "honey," "darling," "baby, baby"
and, lover, I will sip at that sweetness,
all engines firing.
But never come in
for a landing.

### A Piteousness of Doves

My mourning dove is a dollop
of sadness as she lifts her belly
up into the high branches and
onto the balcony rail. Her cooing
haunts the air. Tell me: have you
ever seen a pair of them, entwined
at the ringed necks, together in nature?

### An Exultation of Larks

Juliet hears the nightingale while Romeo
knows the lark's song fails to stop time
but urges all things forward.

For instance, their deaths.

# Deathbed Proof

Spine-straight as a child awakened
out of nightmare, you're captured
here, agog, and without your camera:
the mouth that once fastened
onto the world like a sea anemone
now f-stopped at a speed
that swallows light. How many times
had you commanded us to hold a pose
while you dithered with a filter
or switched lenses. None dared
disobey your starched and tailored
arm imperiously gesturing: "Stand. There."
And we moved, and stood.
Crisp, once, in all things, your lank body
now lost in the fuzzy outlines
of a hospital gown. No contrast,
so it's hard to tell where you leave off
and the bed begins, though we know
it's cranked up as high as you can bear.
How you used to shoot
from that bony hip, literally, in the city,
among strangers, so as not to offend
or get trashed by ones whose faces
rose up later in the developing bath,
intimate as any family or friend.
Your life teemed, a tide pool.
Ah, but here's your end: the blurry focus
of a child astir, her bleak cry for a glass of warm
milk the night of a thunderstorm.

# Day Lilies

In fierce rain they open like starfish
clinging to slick rocks in tide pools,
like a child's splayed hands counting to ten,
a fiery salamander's mouth,
tangerine umbrellas blown
inside out in the wind.
                              But in a vase
the next day they seize up like insects
the spider has sucked dry.

What am I doing here but arranging for death?

IV

# The Zoo at Night (2)

The kiddie tram has hushed itself (*choo-choo*)
so that the elephants' quiet hoovering,
gleaning straw bits left behind on the ground,
and their shuffling, the sound of elephant skin
abrading elephant skin as they huddle,
draw us to their lonely enclosure. A lynx paces.
The hyena rolling onto her back solicits
her mate. But he stares at us, indifferent.
When will you reach for me again in passion?
Morning, and I'll take back the question. Put
you on the spot, I know. I'll edge over
to my side, sleep curled up, barely breathing,
in the shape you find most appealing—that of the treed
koala wrapped up in herself, claws retracted.

# The Entrance of Beauty

I read Cavafy and think about beautiful men,
which means I am thinking about you.
What must it be like to enter a room
and watch eyelids flicker like moths,
gazes adjusted up or down, pooling
at the throat, your glorious throat,
as if it's some safety zone. It's not.
Because then you'll start to speak
even the most unremarkable words,
and mesmerized by the movement
in your larynx, the Adam's apple
floating up and down, protruding,
disappearing, the men and the women
in the room will lose their last thought,
a thought that will ascend to a corner
where wall meets ceiling, and, peeved,
hunch there like the pet we take
for granted, until it's time to go home.
And if not with you—the thought
will be fetched, examined, found
unfamiliar. And those who had it
will recognize an unredeemable loss
as if time had struck twice: the hour
in exile from their own forgotten bodies,
the hour they longed for yours.

# Yellow Sweater

The fleet was in, and we were aging—
desperate, in fact, but not self-deluded.
I wore red lipstick; my friend, a yellow sweater.
Goldfinch and pomegranate. Pouty,
voluptuous, and having none of it,

so that when the young sailor listing
to our side of the pavement
on Columbus reached out to finger
the bright raveling along the edge
of her collarbone she screeched
like some forest hag.

He held up his palms the way
animals display their soft
undersides in surrender, careful,
still, to lock a thumb around his Guinness.

But she kept screaming
as perhaps she hadn't screamed
the night her would-be rapist,
crouching on the fire escape,
entered her apartment—

iron grating collapsed on a hot
night, window ajar. She claimed
that time she'd talked him out of it.
Some quiet lines about illness.
She was younger then,
a better liar.

The sailor vanished into the crowd,
the fog, after tacking his way
down the block.
On the street now people
were giving us the wide berth
accorded the stink of homeless women.
The circle drawn around us
was fretted with fire.

# Too Soon

We drank cold sake out of small wooden boxes,
sake spilling onto porcelain plates, just denser
than water, and by such a slight valence, the weight
of it rested on my tongue like words I'd wanted
to say to make you my lover. You took up the huge
bowl of soup and drained it, and in a half boast, half
apology, told me this is how they drink it in Japan—
something I knew, having been there before you,
having strolled alone in the empress's iris garden after
an April snow.
           That morning, loaded down, the new
cherry blossoms nearly froze, but then the slush,
the icy water, ran into the gutters, impossible
not to step in on the way underground. The mouth
of the subway rider in the seat opposite was cupped
in a white paper mask against contagion. And in
the garden, the green flags of the purple
iris—tended by kneeling women in cloth bonnets,
faces shaded from the sun—were still furled.

# On a Scale Of

You whistle to the parrot in the florist's shop
and he whistles back, and you keep up this shrill
conversation of whistles past the B of A
and onto Castro Street where it fades into traffic
though I think the bird must be whistling still
over the loopy orchids, purple and white,
hanging their heads in the window, solo,
or in clusters, almost animal themselves,
like the internal organs of some faerie beast—
that being your kind of beauty, your nose's
asymmetry, your past full of wailing
and whistling, the writhing of a damaged
liver, the music box of a broken septum.
If you were to lope in the other direction
every beggar on the street would reach out
for you, and not only for the money,
calling out to you "Man," like the most intimate
nickname for you and you alone.
You live one story above their heads,
and should the earth heave you back
onto the streets again you'd know
just how to stick out your hand.
On a scale that spans Wilbur and Bukowski
you're so close to Bukowski you can
smell his booze breath six feet under,
while I've been dilly-dallying with meter
and nurturing a secret ambition
to be a lady who lunches in Connecticut,
speaking French as Madame Goot
taught us in her nasal Ukrainian voice,

peering over crescents of reading glasses
the way you do sometimes, searching
9/11 conspiracies on the Internet.
Madame would not have approved of you.
We second generations were stumbling
into Culture while our fathers drove buses,
sorted mail, got maimed at the American
Can Factory—Cyrano, *Le Bourgeois Gentilhomme*.
We memorized Verlaine ("Les sanglots longs /
Des violons / De l'automne / Blessent mon Coeur / D'une
longeur / Monotone"). Some of us would even marry
dentists. So *excusez-moi* if at times
I appear to be shocked, shocked to be in love with you,
headed, as I had been, for a different fate:
suburban convent redolent of Lysol and bergamot,
with spouse, or without. Nuns and businessmen
worship images. They're manicured, clipped
so clean that sometimes, at night in bed,
when I wake up to your talon scraping my leg,
my ankle, or to your brute, untrammeled snoring,
I have to remind myself that you do know how to whistle,
and most beautifully too.

# Fonder

I awaken to the rough sex of boxcars
coupling, uncoupling, having fallen asleep
to the soughing of mourning doves, putty
dollops with pure voices, their rodomontade
of loss. On the back road someone's driving
up and down, his amped-up bass line drubbing
my peace. Soon we'll see each other after
our longest absence. Our hair will have grown
to our napes, and I wonder if you'll be
wearing clothes I'll find familiar in shape
and smell, and if we'll kiss more awkwardly
than the time you risked my first refusal.
I surprised you then with my open mouth.
Which of us will startle into intimacy?

Which of us will startle into intimacy,
into a kind of half-awakening,
as the breath of a few resident cows
on a moonless night stirred me out of dark,
impatient thoughts and made me laugh
at my own pretensions. The beasts harrumphed,
and in their fairy tale I was the fool
who traded one of them for magic beans
and a beanstalk jutting into the clouds.
There was the deep grass, all a ruminant
could ever need. Our love's terrestrial,
even grounded, where we might safely graze.

Even grounded, where I might safely graze,
I long to stir things up. Can frenzy be

behind us? For instance, your wild dancing?
I don't mean just self-parody, you vamping
to a Prokofiev suite, me laughing
at your antics. I mean, dear, bump and grind,
slow-dance lust, everything short of fucking
on the dance floor. And this display in public,
since your face is like a carnival mask—
a satyr's smile extending ear to ear
beneath that aquiline nose, however
broken. For too long you've avoided things
bacchanalian. Dance with me, lover.
We can do it without drugs, stone sober.

We can do it without drugs, stone sober
though I'm likely to add red wine to the mix.
You know me—a maenad from way back
but never one who went so far as you.
Well, as they say, we both have histories
we revisit now and then. Mendocino,
for example, the bar and dancehall
that you drove me to—closed up (it was morning).
You'd arrive there from the city years ago,
chasing pussy. Your palpable nostalgia
made me queasy. A certain little Irish
girl was often cited: her house, her child.
I thought, "too much information." Is there
such a thing as retrospective jealousy?

Such a thing as retrospective jealousy
wastes too much bile, I know. I'm in detox
from that stuff, though truth be told I can't quite
get enough of yours, feigned or real. A man
comes up in conversation and you need
the who, the what, the when. Soon I'll run out

of stories and invent like Scheherazade,
keep you poised on that delicious fulcrum
between having and desire. (Read Carson's
*Eros* for the *analyse du texte*.) Love,
now let's be serious. I promise not
to play you for a fool. I ask the same
of you. In my presence you will always be
(read Donne) the center of my universe.

Read Donne. The center of his universe
was fixed as he went voyaging. For us
the shoe is, so to speak, now on my wayward foot.
Old homebody, you won't consider
Italy or even Greece. Wanderlust
is in my genes (unlike the other kind,
residing in my jeans, soon to be quelled).
But there is that phrase of yours—"go with"—
you use a lot, in fact, invited me that way
to our first concert date. *Go with, go with,*
*whither thou go with* I wish you'd say.
Although for now these absences provoke
more poetry than our propinquity. Donne,
that errant metaphysical, once proved it.

The errant metaphysical once proved
a perfect landscape for desire: the soul
and body first removed, then joined back up
in perfect symmetry. But impatient
with duality, I'd rather sidle
up to you in Union Station, pull you
to me. I've longed for you so long no
witty trope will do. Let's get to the hotel—
an imperfect room awaits; we will fit

inside of it, inside ourselves, each other.
The medium is distance, the method,
*eros*. Yet I'd rather be in your arms,
here, than writing poems about you, alone,
awakening to the rough sex of boxcars.

# My Sister and I Are Having the Same Dream

Long after nights of arm-tickling across the chasm
between our twin beds, after all the shared illnesses
of childhood—spiking fevers doused in crystalline alcohol,
such pungent, icy baptisms,

after the honeyed scabs of measles and of falls,
years of being mistaken for the other, bowl-cut
bangs fringing wide foreheads, our matching dresses
(until one grew breasts), years of pleasing teachers
with our patterned decorousness,

there came the years of not speaking while the young
warriors pitched tents outside the forbidden city,
each of us carried off, eventually, to the other's chagrin
(*How could you go with him?*)

and now quite detached, a continent between us,
over and over the same nightmare:

an unlocked door about to open, some force making its way in,
a loose chain jangling like a charm bracelet, unlatched,
butterfly hinge molting,
blind knob twisting,
deadbolt un-thrown—

each in her own house, invaded, alone.

# Reading Loop: The Sibyl at Cumae

*For Larry Levis, in memoriam*

You, begetter of elegies, loose-limbed, always waving goodbye—
I'll drink early this afternoon in your memory.
I'll drink deep as I once feared to, seated at your feet.

They've captured you, *rara avis*, in the infinity of a video loop, the unimaginable
immortality of your sensuous mouth, eyebrows like crows
angled in the winter fields that surrounded us

evoked now in this abomination: a small window on the Internet,
a talking holy card. And you, caged within it, like the Sibyl at Cumae
wishing for her death. *I want to die.* You wished wrong. We all do.

Oh to hell with chatty ladies—dry beans shaken up in hollow jars.
You with your sparse hair falling into your eyes, those lighthouses—
who'd blame you for dogging girls still full of juice, leggy and impossible?

Then, on your motorcycle in the blink of an eye you'd high-tail it
out of there into the dark wood. Someone shuffled cards awkwardly,
someone broke open another Jim Beam. The woman you stole

from my friend hugged your waist like a laurel tree. Rapacious god,
to whom we would cling, all of us, as you drove yourself down.
Better that, though, than the Sibyl's withering, her caged voice grown

reedy, nearly inaudible. Larger than life the whisky-palsy of your hand
reaching for the morning's first coffee as you refused the polite banter
of mentoring. You slurred to me, "Well, of course you're all talented."

I replay that meeting, as I'd imagined it, while now thirsty students
beg for another round—even as foam billows, slides down their frosty
glasses, even as I play the bar wench filling orders again and again.

*Remember me?* They write from the foothills of the Appalachians,
from the Big Island. I do. I do remember them. One, your distant
cousin, comes around to remind me how, in your orbit, off-course,

I never spoke my desire but grew angry as the young woman
you were fucking slid into our booth at the Fox Head, cuddling
beside you, interrupting our talk of divorces and other failures

and I hardly knew what I wanted: to be her, to be you, not to be?
By then I had shriveled into nonentity, could have ended my life
any day had I merely the courage. Instead, I kept up the banter

of my bloodless poetry. Years later I can say I "studied with" you.
More to the point, I recognize your hot throat disappearing
into the open shirt collar on that last book jacket, the first name

of the photographer—the young woman I envied? And you,
dead nearly a decade, while I go on, exhuming you in my pettiness,
teacher I hardly knew, lover I never had, wild avatar of *duende*.

That still photo's nothing compared to this video of your public reading
my computer can replay anytime, obsessively. You perch in a corner
of my screen where I can control the volume, freeze the image

of your brief disappearance from the frame as you reach for a water glass,
tiny as the thimbleful of water you imagined in the Sibyl's cage:
the absence of your presence felt eternally, and even now.

# Mating Dance

No fewer than four peacocks spreading their wealth
on the walkway out of the zoo at sunset—
six feet across, a display nearly that high,
they pivot and strut like Philadelphia Mummers
marching in parade—all spokes and turquoise plumes
with purple eyes, one even balanced on the roof,
emitting terrible squawks. But there's only one peahen in sight,
and she, desperate to be lost in faulty camouflage
among the flamingos in their paltry little pond.

As, at a party, the woman flees her unwelcome pursuer,
two full glasses in hand spilling over his sleeves,
and I think how beautiful is his desire to please her
just this once, and how foolish these birds appear
as they snap their feathers back into a tail,
a compact fan, brushing the sidewalk in rebuke
to the whole filthy primate world, the man
tugging at his own cuffs now, as if he could pull them down
so far they would cover even his bitten cuticles in shame.

# Prey

The two mountain lions unfurled their long bodies
and leaped down from the highest metal shelf—
from which they'd ignored us, diffident at day's end,
to pace back and forth, now so close their fur seemed
to catch and ripple as it brushed the bars: They had seen
the man approaching at half-height, rolling along
the path in his wheelchair, and never took their eyes off him.

The man told us it was like this in every zoo, that the big cats
craved him, as if they knew. And riveted,
we watched their fascination as he passed again and again
in front of their cage as if to provoke them
or to surge in the strength of his own freedom there.

You kept saying how they sensed he was the weakest
one of us. And I thought of all the times on the trail
where mountain lion postings warned of danger
how you'd try to tease me out of my fears.
                                        But how
could I rise up, hands in the air, larger than life,
and cast a shadow that would send them packing?
Instead, I would follow my own image as it rolled
from eye to eye, like a child's toy, while I stood still
and waited for the paw on my nape, the scalping.

# Eclipse

You claim no one ever warned you
about looking directly at a solar eclipse,
so this afternoon while the neighborhood
contorts to view it backward,
or through a glass darkly,
or via intricate lenses
at the hilltop observatory, or while
they strain the plangent light
through a kitchen colander
to make satisfying shadows
on the ground, you stare
nakedly at the startling corona
forming around the moon
while all the birds go crazy.

Then you return home to me,
eyes burning, head pounding,
and oh god, I fear
you could have been blinded, then and there.

Each day I curse your recklessness
as I find your cell phone in a pile
of clothing, your reading glasses
in some corner, and as I turn off the burner
on the stove left on again, I recall
how, as a boy of ten, on a dare,
you once dashed across
a busy road where a car threw
you into the air thirty feet, broke
many bones, smashed your skull,

sent you into a coma for days—

you, so full of light, into darkness.

And now you walk among us.
Whole. You beat the drugs, the drink,
the sense that no one ever loved you.
Then what, my darling, could eclipse you?

# The Buddhas of Bamiyan

*The Silk Road, Afghanistan, March 2001*

I had no business caring about their demise:
no Buddhist, I—my desire seems infinite.

Yet those days when I heard the great stone buddhas
in their niches would be blown apart

I had delusions of stopping their destruction:
with money, with letters, with prayer.

Later it seemed no different from marching down Market
in a brace of one hundred thousand peacemakers,

shouting, making steel ring, making concrete hum
with our chants of *No more war! No blood for oil!*

while the city's homeless men looked on, smoking
in the doorways of closed shops, pausing

in their shadowy alcoves, as the stone buddhas
had paused in theirs for centuries,

impassive beside the routes of trade,
rebuking all the preoccupations of human will

with their stony presence.

# Our Road

*You took your hands off the wheel*

So hot, the asphalt was melting back into black ooze,
the thick tar of origins

The sharp hush of air brakes recalled the dusty gravel
of runaway truck ramps,

how breakneck, downhill, could be reversed
by veering off-road

*You took your hands off the wheel*

A guardrail, sharp glinting aluminum
bending as the road bends,

would ensure a pause only
before the plunge into the dark valley

Nearby, the laughter of people tubing
the wild rapids in old tires—

they had found uses for objects that had failed
them in another element

*You took your hands off the wheel*

Not for long, but at freeway speed—
a small stone thrown up then

could split the windshield like a glacier
calving, like an earthquake fault

and the fault is never in the stars
but in ourselves, my love

These reckless acts, these choices:
I'm as weary of reasons

as I am of regrets churning up
road dust      Instead, tell me what

it was like for you to try, again and again,
to cast your life into a fierce wind

only to have it spit back at you, a shower
of grit and sediment

Because when you take your hands off
the wheel, with me beside you,

you take me down too, and I'm not yet done
with this imperfect life.

V

# "Report a Problem with This Poem"

*(As noted on the Poetry Foundation website)*

This poem isn't meant for you or for anyone, really—
hairpin scratches in wet clay, hardly cuneiform,
whatever came to mind then left as quickly.

Resistant, like a child whose fist clamps around
a forbidden piece of candy, so melted now
into shapelessness the child licks the lines of his palm

and thrusts it at your face. "There, all gone."
And yes, you could pretend to be a palm reader
polishing up your own carnival act:

"I see the acrid emptiness of our era, the oblique
impossibility of meaning, and how you've caught
it here in vivid fragments, dragon scales

and a shopping list. I see how it eats its own tail,
its head finally up its own ass, and that is risky
and altogether wonderful." Go along with the gag,

agree that the emperor's in Armani or Ralph Lauren
while his sorry little bag of nuts is swinging
gently in the wind as he struts the runway.

Take a thousand lie detector tests, fail everyone one.
No matter: the operator's in on it. When the poem is read
to a full house, the audience holds its collective breath,

asphyxiated. Polite applause will follow. A learned
article or two. But you? It's like being burglarized

in reverse: Nothing's missing, nothing's rearranged;

still, you're feeling, well, ripped off. You could pull on
your smug mask—hooded eyes, bitten lip, collar
way up to hide your limp neck hairs, un-thrilled.

Or, you could report a problem with that poem.

# "Beautiful Contrivances" in the Sex Life of Orchids

Raise my foot up to your lips.
Drink from a lady's slipper
in the loamy woods. Orchids sip
from the air while they counterfeit
bees' genitals, all warm and fuzzy,
in order to get laid. Other flowers
find a way to do it for themselves.
Not these. The *Catasetum*, for example,
forms a slingshot to launch its wad
onto the back of an insect
go-between. Others are subtler,
their scent mimicking pheromones
to lure besotted drones into a room
full of petals. Like Indiana Jones
the males find the one passageway
to escape, a route that takes them
through a sticky pollen trove.
And shall we call this love? Or what
we all were promised once—a hedge
against death: nervous prom date
fastening the floppy white bracelet
of orchids onto her bony wrist.

# Fumée d'Ambre Gris

*After the painting by John Singer Sargent (1880)*

Intoxication of the self—one's own fingers
spreading the tent wide.

Exquisite solitude, incense rising, as when
the little altar boy swung the censer
at high mass. Everything fainting-white:
lilies creaming at the stamen tips,
the solar host held aloft while the priest
seemed to fall backward in ecstatic adoration;
white surplices and wimples, beads pearling
in darkened hands.
         So much white too
in Sargent's painting where any smear of color
teases: an orange sleeve, kohl-rimmed eyes,
red mouth and nails, the painter's signature
silver gleam on the *noli me tangere* chain
across her breast and on the daunting *fibulae*,
those weaponized brooches that hold
the loosening robes in place as she inhales
smoke rising from the coals of ambergris
burning in the brazier.

What leviathan expelled this?
What rough seas were sailed to find
ambergris tumbled in the trough
or flung up on a beach when the whale
had no more use for it, when it had grown
and graveled in the belly of the beast,
building, building to be heaved—
ah, sweet relief—into the wave?

# The Fascicles of Emily Dickinson

First of all, such a fussy word—little bundles
of nerve sewn up and plunged in a trunk,

sewn with a needle that must have pricked
her, and how she must have sucked her finger

promising herself—next time—a thimble, as the blood
ran down into a starched cuff. Mostly,

though, I'd say she went bareheaded
into the storm, like a scrimshaw etcher

on a surging deck—one eye out for leviathan,
the other trained on a tiny fistful of ivory.

# My Mother in the Eye of the Storm

What's landfall if not the trough of her frown,
spume of her word-spray? The winds have shifted,
barrier fences near the dunes torn down,
a berm breached, reeling seabirds all lifted
into the upper air, far from the hands
that fed them. I have drawn back from the rail
of the roiling ferry, her reprimands
stinging my ears like salt spray. Here's the tale
belowdecks: she's not evil, though we abandon
her, adrift now for nearly a century—
and there's room in her lifeboat for just one.
Take your place, mother, head for the calm sea,
so unfamiliar. I give your vessel a shove
with my battered oar, and something like love.

# Blue Tooth

I can't tell the schizophrenics
        from the cell-phone users anymore:

everyone talking
into the air.

        *And who is the third who walks*
*always beside you?*

Look, I'm trying to be rational here.
I ended a friendship once
over angels. My friend
believed in them.

All I could summon
was a chitinous wing,
a clamshell and its shadow.

Some hold them up to their ears,
then bring them close to their mouths
as if talking back to the sea.

Some gesture wildly
at a building, a tree, or
as if in the orchestra pit, conducting.

But from the theater's front row I saw the wires
        attached at the base of her spine

so that she flew always tilted forward, just a little,
   so unlikely up there,
   so cast down

as if still pining for the ground.

# Ground Note

Twilight, and those with a place to go
had already gone there, those
with someone waiting were measuring
flour or words, switching channels
so as not to annoy. The animal
came from lower ground beneath
the raised parking lot, and I took
her for a dog, big as a wolfhound,
until her clatter closed in: hooves
on asphalt, the panicked autism
of the untamed. A deer, off-course.
There was no way to flag her down.
She made for the tree line but first
butted up against the chain-link fence
they'd just unrolled and staked—
not once or twice, but ringing along
its length, as she fought her way. And not
like bells, not like any kind of song.

# Near Capitol Reef, Utah

A scorpion sting felled Ivey May Holt,
three months old. Soon (it was 1895) thereafter
the farm flooded over, and childless,
the Holts moved on—where, I don't know.
But here's their fallow orchard across the road
from petroglyphs the Anasazi struck into a wall
of rosy sandstone a thousand years ago.
Though Ivey May never got to trace those
tiny big-horned sheep, hunters with bows,
medicine men carved into rock,
with her pink fingertip, or to hold a hot flint
up to her lips and blow the fire back into it,
she had her season.

# Pears in Winter

They have my shape, my skin: matte,
roughened and mottled, etched in brown scars,
tiny skid marks that scarcely break the surface.

Beneath the seeming bruises, a pale-green
presence persists. So that, nearing solstice,
I grow content to wait, as the amaryllis waits,

its pear-like bulb plunged in topsoil,
its come-hither leaf-finger reminding me
to turn to the light, what light there is now,

just a few hours of it. I palpate the pear's
woody stem, shriveled as a crone's nipple,
though not to check for disease,

as we do, but to test for the sweet certainty
of ripeness. And it will come, surging
from the mealy flesh, dribbling down the chin,

whiskered old chin.

## NOTES

"Atlantic City": The Sidhe in Irish legends are fairy nobility
  often depicted riding on horseback in the sky.

"Reading Loop: The Sibyl at Cumae": The Cumaean Sibyl
  resisted Apollo's advances, even though she had promised
  to surrender her virginity to him in exchange for eternal
  life. So the god punished her by giving her eternal life, but
  without eternal youth. She withered into an extreme, awful
  old age and grew so tiny she could barely be seen in the cage
  to which she'd been forever confined. "I want to die," was
  the answer she gave when asked what she most wanted.

"'Beautiful Contrivances' in the Sex Life of Orchids": The
  quoted phrase "beautiful contrivances" has been attributed
  to Darwin.

## In the Prairie Schooner Book Prize in Poetry series

Cortney Davis, *Leopold's Maneuvers*

Rynn Williams, *Adonis Garage*

Kathleen Flenniken, *Famous*

Paul Guest, *Notes for My Body Double*

Mari L'Esperance, *The Darkened Temple*

Kara Candito, *Taste of Cherry*

Shane Book, *Ceiling of Sticks*

James Crews, *The Book of What Stays*

Susan Blackwell Ramsey, *A Mind Like This*

Orlando Ricardo Menes, *Fetish: Poems*

R. A. Villanueva, *Reliquaria*

Jennifer Perrine, *No Confession, No Mass*

Safiya Sinclair, *Cannibal*

Susan Gubernat, *The Zoo at Night*

To order or obtain more information on these or other University of Nebraska Press titles, visit *nebraskapress.unl.edu*.